# WORD TRACK WORKBOOK

*Spelltrack Workbook:*
*Spelling Activities for Key Stages 1 and 2*
Laura Cryer
ISBN 1-84312-000-3

*Phoneme Track Workbook*
Laura Cryer
ISBN 1-84312-138-7

# WORD TRACK WORKBOOK

Laura Cryer

 **David Fulton** Publishers

David Fulton Publishers Ltd
The Chiswick Centre, 414 Chiswick High Road, London W4 5TF

www.fultonpublishers.co.uk

First published in Great Britain in 2004 by David Fulton Publishers

10 9 8 7 6 5 4 3 2 1

David Fulton Publishers is a division of Granada Learning, part of Granada plc.

Note: The right of Laura Cryer to be identified as the author of this work has been asserted by her
in accordance with the Copyright, Designs and Patents Act 1988.

Copyright © Laura Cryer 2004

*British Library Cataloguing in Publication Data*
A catalogue record for this book is available from the British Library.

ISBN 1-84312-137-9

Designed and typeset by Kenneth Burnley, Wirral, Cheshire
Printed and bound in Great Britain

# Contents

# Introduction

Word Track contains photocopiable tracking activities intended to support and reinforce correct spellings of words in the context of the sentence, enabling the learner to work on spellings without anxiety.

Without memory we cannot learn. Without focusing on active methods of learning we cannot improve our ability to memorise and hence to learn. Word Track supports the activities in the Word Track CD-ROM which is an easy-to-use CD-ROM with full audio support and configurable display options published by SEMERC/Granada Learning. Word Track is suitable for use with pupils at Key Stages 2 and 3 as well as with all learners who have particular problems memorising spellings and reading unknown words.

Word Track activities concentrate attention on the letters and sounds (phonemes) of words set within a meaningful context of the sentence. No one source of information for the reader – phonics, spelling patterns, syntactic, semantic or textual clues – can provide the reader with the means for fluent and accurate word identification. The literate reader has to learn to pull all these strategies together to achieve a fluent and accurate reading of the text. Word Track is designed to encourage scanning a line of type to improve word recognition and visual discrimination skills. The learner does not have to look at each letter individually but needs to be able to scan the line of type for the correct word.

Word Track consists of 180 illustrated sentences which are progressively more phonically complex. The learner looks at and reads the model sentence with a supporting picture, which gives further context clues. He/she then has to track (circle) the correct words in the exact order. The sentence is then written, the learner being encouraged to generate as many words as possible accurately from memory. There are many ways that a teacher and/or user may choose to use the activities, both within the classroom and as a resource away from the main teaching situation.

The sentences are listed separately so that the teacher may decide which sentence the user is to work on.

To sum up, Word Track activities:

- encourage users to check each phoneme using visual discrimination skills and proof-reading skills. The users are encouraged to use their visual skills to recognise critical features of words, for example, shape and length of words, common spelling patterns and words within words.

- support the reading and spelling of high frequency words and easily muddled spellings (sed/said), letter order mistakes (form/from, on/no, saw/was) and confusion over letter formation (dent/bent, bin/pin, bed/deb, met/wet).

- incorporate practising correct spellings by 'look, say, remember, check' strategies.

- support the correct use of punctuation and grammatical awareness as well as provide ample opportunity for discussion and exploration of individual learning styles.

# He feels quite sick.

(He)    They    She    It    fells    (feels)    feles    fills

teels    kwite    quiet    quit    (quite)    sikc    sik    sock

(sick)    sack    (.)    !    ?

*He feels quite sick.*

# Word Track Sentences

## We can hop.

I     We     con     nac     can     cann     pop     hop     poh     .     !     ?

## Sam can dig.

sam     Sma     Sam     can     Can     con     big     dip     dig     .     !     ?

## Tim has a map.

Jim     Tin     Tim     haz     his     has     sah     a     o     nap     map     mag     .     !     ?

## Bob is a man.

Bod     Bob     Bad     Dob     a     iS     is     si     A     a     nan     nam

mam     man     .     !     ?

## Put the bag in the bin.

Pul    Pot    put    Put    the    het    hte    bap    baq    dag    bag

in    no    tHe    the    bim    dim    bun    bin    biu    .    !    ?

## She has got a red bag.

Seh    She    Shee    haz    his    has    got    pot    qot    A    a

rod    reb    red    ned    bab    bag    big    dag    .    !    ?

## Tom is sad.

Tim     Tom     tom     lom     si     so     is     sab     sob     sad     sed     .     !     ?

## The cat can sit on my lap.

Ve     The     the     cot     can     cAT     cat     cal     con     can     ist     sat     sitt

sit     no     on     mi     ym     my     MY     tap     pal     lap     top     lop     .     !     ?

# Can Ben fix the van?

Con     Can     Cen     Ben     Bin     ben     den     ficx     ficks

fix     ve      his     the     fan     ven     vann    van      than     .     !     ?

# Did you have fun on the bus?

Dib     DiD     Did     Bit     yuo     you     yoo     had      haev    have     haf

fun     fum     fnu     in      on      the     The     dus      buz     bus     buss     .     !     ?

## She cut her chin when she fell.

Sne    Shee    She    she    kut    cut    CUt    cutt    her    here

har    hcin    chiNN    chin    shin    wen    wehn    when    see    she    seh    fil

tell    fell    fel    .    !    ?

## I like your big red ring.

I    i    lick    love    like    you    yore    your    yaw    dig    dip    bip

big    reb    redd    red    reB    rign    rung    ronq    ring    .    !    ?

## I got this from the junk shop.

I    i    pot    qot    jot    gof    got    thise    this    thiz    form    fron    forn    from

thE    het    the    jukn    gunk    jump    junk    chop    ship    shop    shog    .    !    ?

## I wish I was rich.

i    I    wich    mush    with    wish    I    wos    woz    woas    was    rith    rish

rush    rich    .    !    ?

## The shop sells fish and chips.

Ve    The    the    shot    chop    shoq    shop    seels    seld

sell    sells    sills    fich    fihs    fish    and    ond    anb    ships    fish    chops

chips    .    !    ?

## The fox was quick.

The    the    box    fix    focks    fox    tox    was    saw    is    qick

quike    quick    .    !    ?

# I sing when I get in the bath.

i    I    ai    sign    sing    song    sagn    wen    wehn    when    I    i

pet    get    got    am    no    in    the    teh    dath    both    bath    .    !    ?

# She said yes and then said no.

She    she    Shee    sed    said    siad    jes    yes    yas    and    anb

ven    them    then    said    sed    saib    on    no    one    .    !    ?

## I think you should stop doing that.

i    I    thick    think    thing    yoo    you    yoe    shoulb    should    shud

sop    stop    sotp    stog    doeing    doig    doing    fat    thet    that    .    !    ?

## The path is much too long.

The    the    het    poth    pach    path    qath    IS    is    aS    so    muth

must    much    to    too    two    at    log    lang    logn    long    .    !    ?

## Dad looks slim.

Dab     Dad     Ded     lucks     loocks     looks     slIm     slim     slime     .     !     ?

## The tap drips all day.

the     The     TeH     top     taq     tap     tip     dirps     drisp     brips

drips     oll     all     al     today     bay     daye     Day     doy     day     .     !     ?

## He drops the cups with a crash.

He  eh  he  brops  drops  drip  drosp  the  hte  thee

THe  cups  cusp  cips  cuqs  with  mith  wich  A  o  a  carsh  crach

crash  cash  .  !  ?

## Are you in a rush to get there?

Aer  Are  Ar  yoo  you  your  in  In  no  a  A  ruch  rush  rich

get  ot  to  ti  To  pet  qet  get  the  three  there  their  .  ?  !

# The flag was flying for her birthday.

The   A   flog   frog   flag   flop   was   is   fling   flyig

flying   four   for   the   her   here   birthday   dirthday   birthbay   .   !   ?

---

# He could stand on his hands.

Hee   She   He   he   cood   cuold   could   stan   sand   stond   stand

on   in   no   his   hiz   has   hands   hads   nand   hads   .   !   ?

## I can see a slug on the plant.

I    i    con    can    cin    sea    see    a    A    sulg    glug    slug    slup    on

no    AN    tha    the    palnt    pLAnt    glant    plant    pant    Plant    .    !    ?

## That raft will drift away.

That    ThaT    thot    ratf    roft    raFT    raft    tarf    wil    woll

WIll    will    dirft    driff    drift    brift    awoy    way    away    awaye    .    !    ?

## I can lift you up.

Can    I    i    you    eye    con    kan    can    lived    lifl    tift    lift

lifte    yoo    you    me    op    up    pu    down    .    !    ?

## Can you swim?

Con    Can    can    uyo    yow    yoo    you    siwm    smiw    SwiM

swim    .    !    ?

## Drink up your milk.

Drik    dink    drinck    brink    Drink    pu    op    up    yoor    you

your    this    drink    mikc    wilk    milk    .    !    ?

## The boys play in the water.

The    Those    bouys    boys    doys    boyes    pay    glay    play

playe    on    in    no    the    teh    warter    water    wawter    .    !    ?

## We went to the golf club.

we     We     want     wet     went     wetn     at     to     it     ve     the

glof     polf     golf     gof     culd     clud     club     clob     .     !     ?

## Would you lend me a pen?

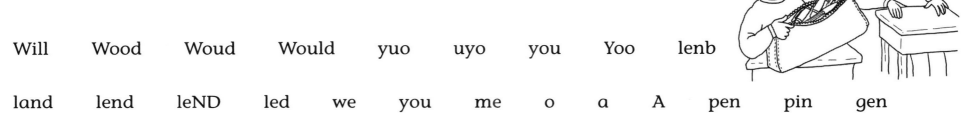

Will     Wood     Woud     Would     yuo     uyo     you     Yoo     lenb

land     lend     leND     led     we     you     me     o     a     A     pen     pin     gen

pan     .     !     ?

## The sun sets in the west.

ThE    The    sonn    suN    sun    sum    in    sest    zest    sETs    sets

no    on    in    iN    The    thee    the    wist    mist    wets    stew    west    .    !    ?

## We must mend the tent.

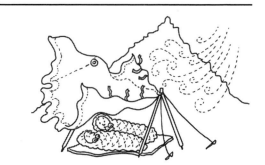

we    We    mut    muts    wust    must    med    menb    mend

wend    The    the    temt    lent    tint    tent    .    !    ?

# I am not very fond of frogs!

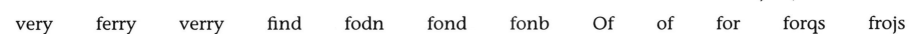

Am     I     ma     aM     am     ton     nit     Nott     knot     not

very     ferry     verry     find     fodn     fond     fonb     Of     of     for     forqs     frojs

frogs     fosg     .     !     ?

---

# Can we have ham with our lunch?

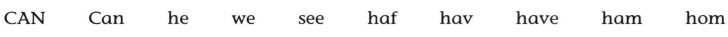

CAN     Can     he     we     see     haf     hav     have     ham     hom

wiv     with     weth     owr     our     owur     luch     luchn     lunch     linCH     .     !     ?

# Put the rest of the junk on the top step.

| But | Pup | Put | pot | the | tha | rets | rust | rests | rest |
| --- | --- | --- | --- | --- | --- | --- | --- | --- | --- |
| for | of | off | tHe | the | gunk | jung | jukn | junk | on | no |
| thE | the | pop | tod | top | setp | step | stop | tsep | steq | . | ! | ? |

# The chimp thumps and bumps.

| The | THE | the | chip | shimp | shrimp | chimq | chimp | thops |
| --- | --- | --- | --- | --- | --- | --- | --- | --- |
| thubs | thumps | thups | anb | and | dumps | bupms | bumps | buwps | . | ! | ? |

## Rick should scrub the sink.

Ric    Rick    RiKc    should    shood    shoud    stum    scub

scrud    scrub    srub    the    The    snik    sink    sick    .    !    ?

## We splash in the pond.

He    We    we    splash    spash    splosh    slosh    iN    in    the    The

pind    ponb    podn    pond    pand    .    !    ?

# The strong man can lift the box.

The THE strange strogn strong stong nam man

mam can con cann loft litf lift lit the het bosx box dox

bosh . ! ?

# There are two eggs in that nest.

THEre Their There The the are arre ar to tow

two too egs esgg eggs eges on in no vat that the a

sten nets nost nest . ! ?

## She does not eat the crust.

He    She    Shee    dose    does    dus    boes    not    nit    ont

eet    eat    ate    the    ve    curst    cruts    crust    crisp    .    !    ?

## He feels quite sick.

He    They    She    It    fells    feels    feles    fills    teels    kwite    quiet

quit    quite    sikc    sik    sock    sick    sack    .    !    ?

## Those lads play out very late.

The    Those    these    dals    slads    lads    lids    lasd    pay    qlay    paly    play

owt    out    wot    very    veri    verry    latte    late    laet    .    !    ?

## I feel safe now that I am home.

i    I    fel    teel    feel    fell    sofe    sefa    safe    save    now    won

vat    thet    that    I    i    ma    am    Home    hoem    homes    home    .    !    ?

# My friend Dave made a good save.

Mi        my        My        firend        fried        friend        frend        Dave        dave        maid        maed

mabe        made        a        gud        goob        good        save        saves        safe        saef        .        !        ?

# It is wise not to drive too fast.

It        it        si        is        it        wize        wise        wies        ont        ton        not

too        to        two        brive        dive        drive        to        two        too        fats        fat        fast        .        !        ?

# I hope you can come on Sunday.

I    i    hop    hoqe    hoep    hope    yoo    you    oyu    con

can    cum    come    on    in    Sundy    Sunday    Suday    .    !    ?

# The mole dug a hole.

the    The    mile    moll    moel    mole    bug    dug    bup

dog    a    A    holl    hoel    whole    holer    hole    .    !    ?

## The whole thing was a bad joke.

The    the    whole    hole    howle    fing    thig    thin    thing

wos    saw    was    a    A    bod    dab    bab    bed    bad    jock    joke    goke

jocker    .    !    ?

## I hope you do not smoke.

i    I    hop    hoep    hoqe    hode    hope    yoo    yo    you

yow    bo    do    dou    nto    nott    not    sock    smock    smoke    .    !    ?

## You can send the bill to my dad.

you    yOo    You    con    cna    can    sed    senb    send    the

dill    bil    bill    ball    to    To    my    mi    am    dad    dod    dob    bab

.    !    ?

## I am in a mess again.

I    i    ma    on    in    am    no    in    a    mes    moss

mess    ness    agen    agin    again    againe    .    !    ?

## Is that your friend at the back door?

Is    as    this    that    then    you    yoor    your    fried    fiend

frienb    friend    at    to    by    the    our    dack    back    dock    bake    dore

boor    door    .    !    ?

## The children walked down the road.

The    Ten    Tin    Two    chidren    children    childen    walks    walkt    waked

walked    done    down    downe    the    a    rode    road    robe    .    !    ?

## The blue team won the toss.

THE    the    The    bloo    blue    bue    dlue    teem    taam

meat    team    one    won    woN    tHe    the    toos    tass    tosss    toss    .    !    ?

## Are you well?

Aer    Are    Arr    yoo    you    wel    well    mell    weel    .    !    ?

# He pushed her off the cliff.

She    He    he    puthed    pushd    bushed    pushed    here    her

heer    of    for    off    the    ve    het    clift    ciff    cliff    ffilc    .    !    ?

---

# Sue waved the flag.

Seu    Sue    Soo    wavd    waived    wave    waved    vawed    the

teh    falg    flap    flop    flag    tlag    .    !    ?

# Helen loves joking with June.

Heln    Helen    Hen    likes    loves    loevs    jocking    goking    joking

wiv    wif    with    Juen    June    .    !    ?

# Pat is hoping to visit me.

Pat    pat    Pet    si    is    iz    hopeing    hopig    hopping

hoping    ot    to    tow    vist    vitit    visit    vsit    me    mee    my    .    !    ?

## The man was choking on a snack.

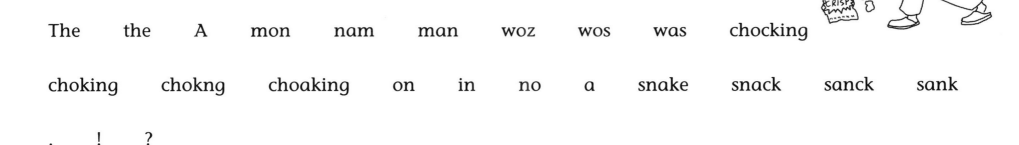

The   the   A   mon   nam   man   woz   wos   was   chocking

choking   chokng   choaking   on   in   no   a   snake   snack   sanck   sank

.   !   ?

## We baked three cakes at school.

Me   We   we   daked   backed   bakd   baked   thee   there

threee   three   cacks   cakes   cokes   to   it   ta   at   shool   scool   school

schole   .   !   ?

## She is ill and may die.

He    She    she    is    so    was    ill    il    lil    and    aND

ond    my    may    miy    diy    bie    di    die    .    !    ?

## I saw the thief creep away.

I    i    was    wos    saw    tHe    the    theef    thefe    thief

cerep    ceerp    creeq    creep    awaye    away    awai    .    !    ?

## Eat fewer sweets if you want to keep your teeth.

Eet    Eat    few    fewer    sweet    swetts    sweets    for    if    yoo

U    you    went    wnat    watn    want    tu    to    kepe    keip    keep    yor

youre    your    teath    teeth    teth    theet    .    !    ?

## That car has three wheels.

That    that    tat    care    carr    car    his    has    haz    there

thre    three    weels    whells    wheesl    wheels    .    !    ?

## Joe cut his little toe on a nail.

Jeo    Joe    joe    cutt    cat    tuc    cut    hiss    his    litle    little

littel    joe    toe    teo    nail    no    in    on    oN    A    a    nale    nail    .    !    ?

## What kind of food do you love?

Wat    What    what    whot    kid    kinb    kind    for    of    off

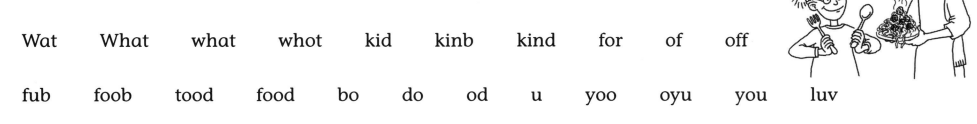

fub    foob    tood    food    bo    do    od    u    yoo    oyu    you    luv

love    .    !    ?

## Start to dig in this part of the garden.

Sart    Strat    Start    ot    to    too    big    dip    dig    in    ni

no    thiz    this    htis    prat    qart    part    for    of    if    the    th    graden

garden    parben    .    !    ?

## Mark will park his new car.

Mrak    Mack    Mark    mill    wil    will    park    dark    parck

the    hiz    his    has    niw    niew    new    wen    cor    carr    care    car    .    !    ?

## We can see the swimming pool.

we  We  can  con  cann  say  se  cee  see  the  The  swiming

swimming  siwming  poll  pull  pool  qool  gooll  .  !  ?

## This is a good book.

this  This  htis  so  iss  is  a  A  gud  goob  pood

good  boock  bock  dook  boook  book  .  !  ?

## The old man had a nice face.

THe    The    THE    owld    olb    dlo    old    mam    man    nam

hod    hab    had    nad    A    a    mice    niec    nice    faec    face    foce    fais

.    !    ?

## We have space for my brother.

WE    Me    We    we    haf    Have    have    hav    spACe    sace

spase    sapce    space    spaic    for    four    Fore    fro    mi    MY    my    may

borther    bother    drother    brother    .    !    ?

## Do small mice like rice?

Do      bo      do      samll      small      smal      saml      mice      wice      mise      mIce

lick      love      like      licke      rice      rise      rICe      riace      .      !      ?

## It is cold in the hall.

It      IT      ti      si      so      is      cobl      cod      kold      colb      cold

iN      in      on      the      THE      hole      hal      hall      holl      .      !      ?

# I have told you twice to stop.

I    A    hav    haver    haea    have    telled    tolb    told

yuo    you    yoo    tise    wtice    twice    too    ot    of    to    sop    stog    stop

step    .    !    ?

# She asked if she could help.

He    She    SHe    Her    aksed    askeb    askd    asked    for

if    of    it    he    shee    she    her    cud    cood    could    coulb

hlep    helq    help    .    !    ?

# I forgot that I am going away.

I    He    frogot    forgt    forgot    foget    vat    that    thaf

I    i    ma    on    am    gowing    going    goinq    gong    way    awy    awye

away    .    !    ?

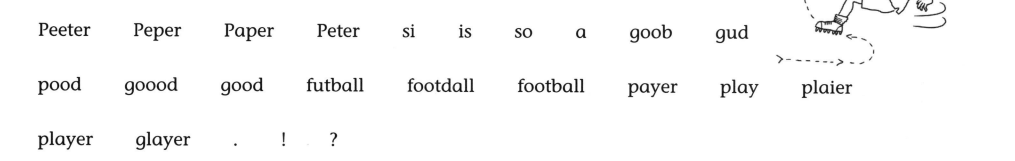

# Peter is a good football player.

Peeter    Peper    Paper    Peter    si    is    so    a    goob    gud

pood    goood    good    futball    footdall    football    payer    play    plaier

player    glayer    .    !    ?

# Call the doctor in the morning.

Coll      Call      Cold      the      dotcor      boctor      docter      doctor

the      in      the      The      mornig      morning      mroning      morming      .      !      ?

# We saw the actor in a play.

we      We      wee      me      was      wos      saw      sor      the      ve

acter      akter      octor      actor      a      no      in      an      a      paly

qlay      playe      play      .      !      ?

## People often read a newspaper.

Peeple   People   Peopel   ofen   offen   often   reed   reab

rdea   read   a   newpaper   wenpaper   newsper   newspaper   .   !   ?

## Please stop spoiling our game.

Pleas   Pease   please   Please   sotp   stop   stoq   step   spoling

sopling   spoiling   hour   uor   our   gaem   game   gane   pame   .   !   ?

# My brother always annoys me.

My     Mi     my     dother     drothre     bother     brother     allway     always

almeys     anoys     annosy     annoys     we     me     you     .     !     ?

# Will you walk and talk with me?

Mill     Will     will     wil     yoo     you     wallk     wark     work     walk     aND

and     anb     tork     talk     tack     wiv     with     we     me     mee     .     !     ?

## Jean is a teacher at our school.

Jeen     Geen     Jean     a     so     is     in     a     techer     teecher

teacher     it     at     to     ower     our     owre     sckool     skool     school     .     !     ?

## I know it is sunny today.

A     I     now     knwo     know     knoo     is     it     ti

is     suny     sonny     sunny     tday     tobay     today     toody     .     !     ?

## Would you like a slice of toast?

Would     Woulb     Woob     yuo     you     uyoo     licke     like     lieke     A     o

slis     a     slys     silice     slice     for     of     off     towst     tots     toast     toats     .     !     ?

## We must not bully anyone.

We     Me     Wee     most     muts     much     must     nit     not     nott

buly     dully     bully     enyone     enywon     anyone     anione     .     !     ?

## Look out for toads on the road.

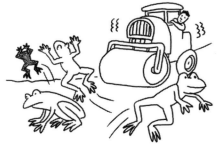

luk    Look    luok    out    owt    of    for    fore    towds    toasd    toads

no    on    in    tHe    the    tHE    roab    rowed    raod    road    .    !    ?

## Will it snow tomorrow?

Mill    Wil    Will    snow    it    to    swom    sown    snow

tomorow    tommorrow    tomorrow    .    !    ?

## His right boot is too tight.

Hiz    His    his    rihtg    rite    right    rigth    boot    doot    booot    is

so    too    to    tite    tiyt    tihght    toght    tight    .    !    ?

## My friend will write tonight.

Mi    my    My    firend    friend    frend    frienb    will    wil    mrite    writ

write    tonigth    tonigt    tonigh    tnight    tonight    .    !    ?

# She came in third in the race.

| He | Seh | She | come | in | cam | came | in | no | therd | thirb | third |

| tired | on | in | no | tHe | the | The | rack | rayce | race | raise | . | ! | ? |

# Fight for what is right.

| Fite | Fight | Feight | Fyight | fof | of | for | wot | what | wahtt |

| so | is | rwight | rigth | right | . | ! | ? |

## Sam threw the stew away.

San      Som      Sam      thew      therm      frew      threw      teh      the      setw

stew      sew      amay      way      away      awaye      .      !      ?

## My brother can dance very well.

Mi      My      my      bother      borthre      brother      con      can      veri

barnce      darnce      dance      veri      very      well      mell      wel      .      !      ?

## She drew a circle with her pencil.

SHE    She    shee    brew    drew    derw    a    A    sircel    circel

sercle    circle    wiv    with    wih    a    the    his    her    pensle    qencil    gencil

pencil    .    !    ?

## The gerbil jumps out of its cage.

The    A    greble    gerble    jerbil    gerbil    junps    jups    jumps

owt    owtt    uot    out    of    for    on    its    kage    cape    caqe    cage    cages

.    !    ?

# Rick lost his balance.

Rick    rick    Rikc    lots    tost    stol    lost    hiz    His

his    balane    dalance    balance    .    !    ?

# George likes ginger cake.

Gorge    Gerge    George    licks    likes    liks    giner    giger    ginger

cake    cacke    caike    .    !    ?

## It was a great tennis match.

The    It    to    it    saw    is    was    so    a    A    grate    geat    graet    great

tennes    tennis    tinnis    mach    math    match    motch    .    !    ?

## The kitchen was filthy.

the    The    Teh    kichen    kitchon    kitchen    saw    was

wos    fithy    filhy    filthy    .    !    ?

## Is the candle on the table?

So   Is   The   a   then   the   candel   cande   candle   no

in   on   the   THe   table   .   !   ?

## I have lost my badge.

i   I   hav   haev   have   lots   my   lost   last   my   mi   bage

dadge   dage   badge   .   !   ?

## Put the fudge in the fridge.

Pot    Put    Pul    the    The    fuge    fude    tudge    fudge    no

the    on    in    ten    the    fidge    fridge    frige    .    !    ?

## Keep the dog in his kennel today.

Kep    Keeq    Keeg    Keep    the    bog    god    dog    on    in

no    hiz    his    kennel    kenell    tobay    today    tobai    .    !    ?

## The girl lost her purple purse.

THE      the      The      his      gril      gerl      girl      lots      lost      last      here

her      har      pruple      purpel      purqle      purple      pors      purrs      purse

gurse      .      !      ?

## My sister fell and hurt her shoulder.

Mi      My      May      sister      siser      sitter      fall      fell      fel      anb      and

hert      hrut      hurt      his      her      herr      showlder      sholder      shoulder

shouler      .      !      ?

# That paint is dry now.

The     That     that     then     payn     pait     qaint     paint     so     is

dyr     bry     dry     nom     won     now     .     !     ?

# He did not try to reply.

She     He     bid     dib     did     on     not     net     tri     try

fry     to     on     repy     regly     reply     .     !     ?

## Mick often tells lies.

Mick     Mike     Mik     ofen     offen     often     lets     tells

liys     leis     lies     .     !     ?

## The ladies were crying.

Ve     The     the     then     ladise     ladies     labies     ledies     were

was     are     weer     cryng     crying     cying     criying     .     !     ?

## The spies were going to prison.

All    The    spes    spies    sepis    speis    wer    are    were

weer    ging    going    goig    poing    to    too    pison    prison    grison    .    !    ?

## My silly brother always copies me.

Her    Mi    My    sily    slily    silly    silli    dother    borther

brother    allways    olwas    always    olways    copes    me    coqies

copies    copes    me    you    .    !    ?

# Babies often cry.

Babies    Badies    Bades    always    ofen    often    oten    cry    cyr

criy    .    !    ?

# The sound from the party was very loud.

The    THE    the    sownd    sond    sound    for    form    the

from    a    the    praty    party    partty    wos    was    is    veri

very    loub    loud    lowd    .    !    ?

## Mum started to shout loudly.

Mom    MuM    Mum    sarted    startd    started    too    to    ot

showt    sout    shout    loudly    loudy    lowdy    .    !    ?

## The cat tried to catch the mouse.

The    Tha    cot    catt    cat    tride    tried    tribe    of    to    fo    coch    cach

catch    cath    the    a    A    mowes    moues    mose    mouse    .    !    ?

## They will be here in half an hour.

He    They    Thay    will    wil    mill    de    bee    be    hear

here    her    in    on    harf    haf    have    half    on    no    an    our    hour

houre    .    !    ?

## That picture is worth millions.

Vat    tat    That    is    piture    pictor    picture    pictore    is

so    as    wroth    werth    worth    milions    millons    million    millions    .    !    ?

## My friend brushes my hair.

My    mi    miy    frend    fiend    friend    frienb    burshes

brushes    brush    mi    my    My    hare    hiar    hair    haire    .    !    ?

## Do not stare at them.

Bo    Not    Do    do    nott    note    not    stares    stair    stare

ot    to    at    then    them    than    .    !    ?

# We paid our fare on the bus.

He    We    WE    pade    gaid    paib    paid    ower    our

hour    fair    fare    faier    no    in    on    the    hte    dus    buss    bus    .    !    ?

# Wash your car with care.

Mash    Wosh    Wach    Wash    yor    your    yoor    cor    carr    car

with    wif    mith    caire    care    cear    .    !    ?

# She wrote a good letter.

She    He    she    hes    rote    wote    worte    wrote    a    the    A

gud    goob    good    jood    leter    litter    letter    .    !    ?

# Dad had to climb into the attic.

daad    Dab    Dad    Bad    hid    hod    had    to    too    cimb    clime

climb    in    on    into    a    the    The    atic    atick    attick    attic    .    !    ?

# Robert hit his thumb.

Rodert    Robret    Robert    it    hit    hitt    hiz    has    his    thum

thumm    thumb    .    !    ?

# Please pay attention.

Pleese    please    Please    Pelease    pay    gay    qay    atention

attension    attention    .    !    ?

## Is the park in this direction?

Is    is    has    the    The    dark    prak    parck    park    on

in    these    this    diretion    dirction    direction    .    !    ?

## Do you want sauce with that?

Bo    Doo    Do    do    yoo    yuo    you    wont    wat    want

sorce    sauce    sawce    wiv    with    wich    vat    thet    that    this    .    !    ?

## The baby can crawl.

THE     The     baby     babey     dady     baby     con     can     cannot

crall     carwl     crawl     .     !     ?

## Laura went into the haunted house.

Lara     Laura     Lora     ment     wet     went     want     into     in

too     the     a     huantd     hauntd     haunted     hunted     howse     houses

houes     house     .     !     ?

## Paul was happy because he won the race.

Pawl     Paull     Paul     Pall     was     saw     hapy     happi     paggy

happy     becase     becos     because     decause     she     he     hee     one

won     now     the     The     a     rase     raec     race     .     !     ?

## Dogs have strong jaws.

Doqs     Dosg     Gods     Dogs     hafe     have     hav     haev     srong

stong     strong     sterong     gaws     jores     gasw     gaws     jaws     .     !     ?

## The thieves took everything.

The    Th    THe    theeves    thieves    theives    thiefs    tuk    tuck

took    evrything    evrthing    everthig    everything    evrething    .    !    ?

## Cut the cakes with those knives.

Kut    Cutt    Cot    Cut    the    a    cackes    cakes    cacks    kaces

wiv    with    these    the    those    nifes    knife    knives    knaves    kives    .    !    ?

## We saw the dolphins swimming.

Me   We   was   wos   saw   the   a   some   bophins   dolphins   dolfins

bolphins   siwming   swimming   swiming   .   !   ?

## I am going to take a photograph.

I   Aye   ma   am   on   gowing   goig   going   poing   tow   it

to   tack   take   tacke   a   the   photgraph   photograph   fotograff   .   !   ?

## Stephen is my nephew.

Stephen    Stephan    Steven    is    so    my    is    mi    nepew

nefew    nephew    .    !    ?

## The child wrote a book.

A    the    The    chid    chilled    chiled    child    write    work    wrote

wrot    a    A    buk    boock    book    .    !    ?

## Look out, she is behind you!

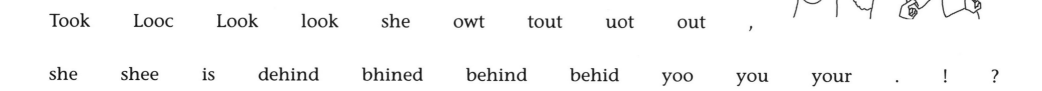

Took     Looc     Look     look     she     owt     tout     uot     out     ,

she     shee     is     dehind     bhined     behind     behid     yoo     you     your     .     !     ?

## Can you find the way home?

Con     Can     Cann     Are     You     you     Yoo     fiend     fined

find     our     the     The     a     waye     way     wai     home     hoem

hm     horme     hone     .     !     ?

# Christopher wants to be a chemist.

Cristofer      Christopher      Christofer      wonts      watns      to      wants      to

it      de      be      bee      a      A      cemist      chemits      chemist      chmist      .      !      ?

# The orchestra played quiet music.

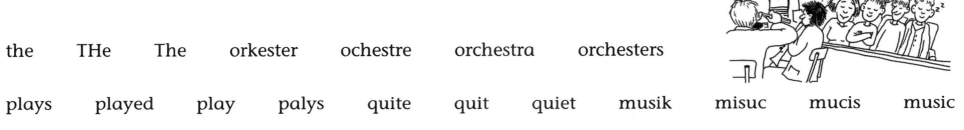

the      THe      The      orkester      ochestre      orchestra      orchesters

plays      played      play      palys      quite      quit      quiet      musik      misuc      mucis      music

.      !      ?

## Bob likes an adventure.

Bod     Bob     Dob     lickes     like     likes     lickes     on     no     an

adventor     adventore     aventure     adventure     .     !     ?

## It was pleasant weather.

It     it     Is     saw     is     was     wos     plesant     qleasant     pleasant

pleasent     Wether     whether     weather     Weather     .     !     ?

# The guide will show us the way.

The     A     that     giube     qide     guibe     guide     mill     will

well     chow     shoe     show     uss     us     uz     the     a     wai     waye     way     .     !     ?

---

# Would you like a slice of bread?

Wood     Would     Woulb     yoo     you     You     lick     like     lice

a     one     silce     slick     slice     for     of     off     dread     bread     bred     .     !     ?

# Ready, set, go!

Redy     Ready     Reddy     gow     set     sett     seet     ready     go

gow     po     qo     gow     .     ,     !     ?

# They wash their hands in water.

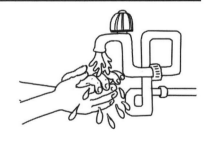

Thay     They     The     wosh     wohs     wach     wash     there     thear     their

hanbs     hands     hanb     on     in     woter     warter     worter     water     .     !     ?

# I have four naughty daughters.

I   i   we   have   had   heav   hav   for   four   fore   fore

norty   naughty   nauhty   dorters   bauhters   daughters   dorters   .   !   ?

---

# The sea was very rough.

THe   Teh   The   the   see   sae   sea   se   was   wos

saw   veri   very   verry   rugh   ruff   rouhg   rough   .   !   ?

# Has she won the match?

Have     Has     has     his     he     she     shee     one     win     won     now

the     tHe     watch     mach     match     macth     .     !     ?

# The woman saw an angry wolf.

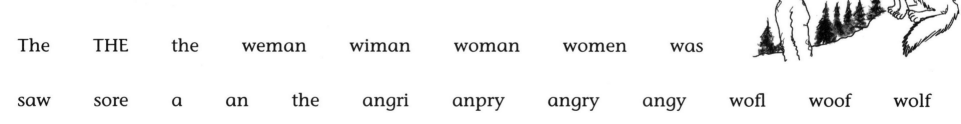

The     THE     the     weman     wiman     woman     women     was

saw     sore     a     an     the     angri     anpry     angry     angy     wofl     woof     wolf

.     !     ?

# The pipes burst last Thursday.

The  THe  They  pips  piqes  pides  pipes  durst  burts

brust  burst  larst  last  lats  tast  Thursday  Thurday  thrusday  .  !  ?

# Helen gets paid on Friday.

Heln  Helan  Helen  is  gets  gets  gest  paib  pade

paid  no  on  in  Firday  Fribay  Friday  .  !  ?

# Shops are often closed on Sundays.

Shogs     Shops     Shop     Chops     ar     are     ofen     offen     often     cosed     closd

closed     on     in     no     Sunday     Sundays     Sunbays     .     !     ?

# Fred gets his pocket money on Saturdays.

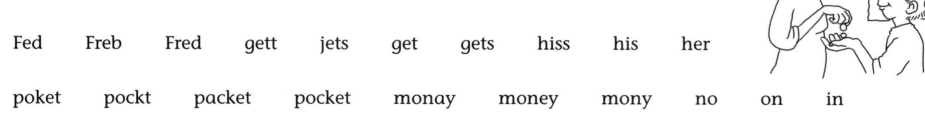

Fed     Freb     Fred     gett     jets     get     gets     hiss     his     her

poket     pockt     packet     pocket     monay     money     mony     no     on     in

Satdays     Satrdays     Saturdays     .     !     ?

## The day before Wednesday is Tuesday.

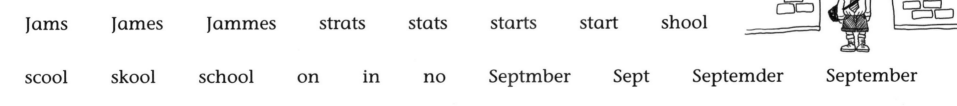

The       Teh       A       the       bay       daye       day       defor       befor       before

bfore       Wednsay       Wednsbay       Wednesday       Wensday       is       so       as       Tuewday

Tuesbay       Tusday       Tuesday       .       !       ?

---

## James starts school in September.

Jams       James       Jammes       strats       stats       starts       start       shool

scool       skool       school       on       in       no       Septmber       Sept       Septemder       September

.       !       ?

# Her birthday is in August.

His     Her     Here     dirthday     birthday     so     in     is

on     in     August     Awgust     Orgust     Auguts     august     .     !     ?

# February is often cold.

Febuary     February     Fedurary     so     in     is     an     offen

ofen     often     cowld     colb     cold     .     !     ?

# My friend is arriving in July.

Mi    May    My    firend    friend    frienb    trend    so    in

is    ariving    arriveing    arriving    on    in    by    Jully    Juliy    july    July

.    !    ?

---

# April is the fourth month.

Aepril    April    Apirl    so    in    is    a    the    on    forth

fouth    fourth    fourht    monch    munsh    month    moth    .    !    ?

85

## Connor is eight years old.

Conor    Conner    Connor    so    as    has    is    eght    ight    eight    8t

ieght    yeers    yeres    years    ears    owl    olb    old    older    .    !    ?

## My sister Emma is forty next birthday.

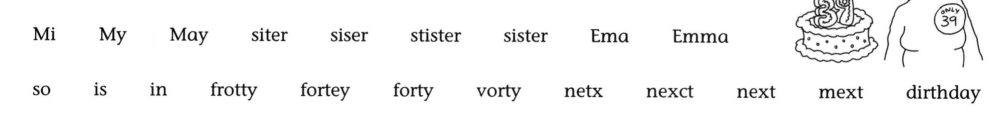

Mi    My    May    siter    siser    stister    sister    Ema    Emma

so    is    in    frotty    fortey    forty    vorty    netx    nexct    next    mext    dirthday

birthday    .    !    ?

## It is only half past three.

In    It    Is    is    so    ownly    onley    oney    only    harf    hafe

halve    half    pats    past    qast    parst    thee    there    free    three    .    !    ?

## Tom caught two fish.

Ton    Tom    Tomm    corght    cauht    caught    corte    too    to

tow    two    fsh    fich    fish    .    !    ?

## Seven enormous creatures ran away.

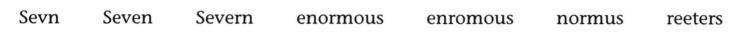

Sevn    Seven    Severn    enormous    enromous    normus    reeters

creatures    creturs    creators    run    ren    ran    ram    way    awaye

away    awaiy    .    !    ?

---

## I have two cousins.

I    You    We    hav    hafe    have    to    tow    two    too    coosins

cousins    cusins    .    !    ?

# Harriet can count to one hundred.

Harriet     Harret     con     cann     can     count     cout     caunt     to     too

won     on     one     hunded     hundred     hundreb     .     !     ?

# There are sixteen different cakes in that shop.

Three     Theer     There     ar     are     arre     sixten     sisteen

sixteen     sisten     diferent     bifferent     different     cackes     cake     cakes

kaces     on     in     no     that     the     chop     shoq     shog     shop     .     !     ?

## We can see five people in that queue.

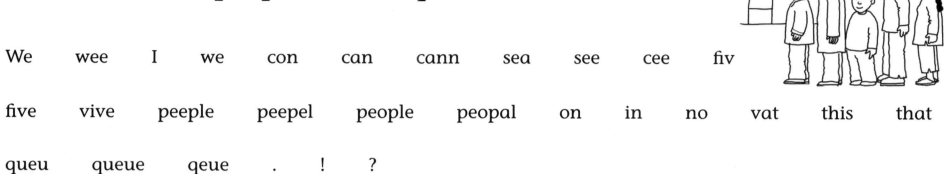

We    wee    I    we    con    can    cann    sea    see    cee    fiv

five    vive    peeple    peepel    people    peopal    on    in    no    vat    this    that

queu    queue    qeue    .    !    ?

## Here comes the number eleven bus.

Heer    Here    There    He    comes    cums    come    hte    the

numder    number    nomdre    elefen    elven    eleven    dus    bus    buss    .    !    ?